Don't get poetry? Don't like poet
will change your mind. F
do not get an

Memorial Device

A Decade of Drinking with Ghosts raises up the lost souls and the
wasted saints. It is a moving and visceral portrait of our lovely
unlovely towns and the lonelier paths we walk down. At times
a lamentation, at others a paean, always, the world comes to
us shining and keening in Gant's prose. Here, we look behind
our locked doors at the pain of fading, imagined futures, yet,
still sensing that in one of those moments where nothing ever
happens, it just might.

Jade Angeles Fitton
author of *Hermit*

Honest and moving poems which turn on a much-needed
light in the dark rooms of our minds; haunted by memory, by
regret and peopled by the politics of this last difficult decade.

Andrew McMillan
author of *Physical*

Complex, humane and melancholic, Gant's voice carries an
important and precious authenticity. These are poems of
bleakness and momentary beauty.

Wendy Erskine
author of *Sweet Home* and *Dance Move*

A Decade of Drinking with Ghosts

Bobby Gant

BOOKS

A Decade of Drinking with Ghosts

Published by Razur Cuts Books (2024), a subsidiary of Nameless Town

razurcuts.com
razurcuts@gmail.com

ISBN: 978-1-914400-74-2

Edited and typeset by Dickson Telfer
Jacket design by stonedart

All photography appears courtesy of the author

Printed and bound by Martins the Printers, Berwick-upon-Tweed

BOOKS

For those who have believed in me,
whether fleetingly or enduringly

Contents

Thirties

They say hell is meeting the person you could have been
Potential on fire, burning as you swill the dregs of youth
The smoke claustrophobic and laced with nostalgia
and quiet desperation
All dying coals flicker with life, threaten to reignite
Does that make the inevitable cold
all the harder to accept?

They say heaven is a place where nothing ever happens
I'm not there yet
Taste as redemption, bitter self-deception eating time
chewing existential crisis on erratic repeat
Haunted
Can we drink to forget
the things that haven't happened yet?

The Internal Ties that Bind / Mary

Sitting in hushed semi-light
too afraid to abandon darkness completely
bewildered by the prospect
of stepping into the light
Afraid of the sacrifice that entails
Selfish beer
self-destructive shot
please and thank you
With a patch over one eye
because only the truly blessed
or the over-confident
should ever want to see – clearly – really see
So
dance
fuck
fight
and help others like you'll never be able to help yourself
The lost embrace semi-light and use solitude to pray
that her tears are never again for you
and that maybe one of *hers*
one day will be

Suicide by Sea / RPWT

Drinking alone on the waterfront
surrounded by ghosts and cracked memories
Poison sometimes rests in a beautiful bottle
as the heft of the sea will testify
And she is here somewhere, somewhere close
among the sound of the waves and the endless faces
She wears her history like a light shawl,
not quite trauma but emotionally distressing
yet she carries it well, maybe too well
I thought of this in an orbit of quiet desperation
Again drinking, again alone
On a morbid afternoon before Christmas
I had no idea of the suffering ahead
Melancholy is supposed to prepare you for happiness
but I missed the last train again
Love is merely an emotional expression of obsession, I
tell myself

One more night of loneliness can't hurt
rooted to this spot anchored by an emotional baggage I
packed in my own head
Ridiculous and false
I wanted it to be false
But somehow there was a real feeling curdling just below
the surface
Nasty and unwanted
Or so it should be
but I didn't want to admit I thrived in this place

Ravaged by a pain beyond words and meaning
addressing the night and the sea
I begged for some sort of clarity
Walking and crawling and hardly moving at all
hounded by conscience
through vomit-soaked streets
There's a romance to this place,
a certain embarrassed charm

I'm getting bold, grown by pain
Searching the whites of every wave
looking for your eyes
You now, you
even though I can't put a name on it
I'm happy here in poverty, happy here in the saddest
thoughts of man
Man only can feel like this
and among sea spray and salty cloud
the truth lands heavy like a loaded dice
I wasn't ready for this
Asleep at the wheel of my own life
it's the perfect way for it to fall,
the perfect way for a man to lose himself
to hopeless love, like in a cheap novel that he'd never
admit to reading
I know you think I must be lost now
but I'm not quite, sinking yes
but sinking somewhere I know

A Moment

That fucking dog is barking again
and for what?
Last two beers in the fridge
pointless observations
all boring
How can you articulate a moment in the dark,
drenched in wedding day wine?
a moment where nothing happened
These chicken wings are old and tough
one beer left in the fridge
A moment cooled by a slight north easterly
barely perceptible at the time
broken conversation and a dozen different accents
a moment where nothing happened
A car horn sounding on the country road
and I sit to ponder
try to think
drink beer
Italian lager
it's all very unimportant somehow
Does she remember the moment?
If not
is it real
or just a figment of a drunken romantic imagination?
Just a moment
a moment where chance
adventure
youth

hope
everything
it all seemed to be there
and be possible
    And then it was over
gone
finished
    Just like a can of beer
only probably even sadder
empty now .
    Life is just made up
of mad little moments
where nothing ever happens
empty now

All Those Rooms

All those rooms
where the big conversations evaporated
hold a part of me still.
That room and that room,
all those rooms.
Hotels and pubs –
cafes and clubs
and every long-forgotten address;
all those rooms.
That part of me that stayed,
left behind in a wash of memories
will stay forever.
That solemn part of me stares forlornly
at a wall of lost time
and wonders
'what happened in the future those people spoke of?'

Cigarette Smoke

Orange juice and newspapers
full of bad news, about
banks and wars,
maybe political scandal.
Full of bad news;
of that I am satisfied,
certain in fact.
Glancing over headlines while the smell
of cigarette smoke
from last night lingers,
telling its own story; a story
that isn't in the morning papers.
Timeless words spoken. The kind
of words which haunt speaker
and heeder alike, for much longer
than the events that led to those words
took to happen.
A play of quick conclusion
but a lasting legacy.
A smile. Did I imagine a smile?
It seems muddled,
a memory out of place.
Just words and cigarette smoke.
You smoked continuously, perhaps
in a bid to calm nerves as the
colossal significance of the moment
dawned on you. Dawned on us both.
Then in the smoky haze

you disappeared. It would be wrong
to say you left, or walked out,
for it was more poignant
and more final than
those descriptions can do justice.
In a cloud of cigarette smoke
and the echo of words spoken,
it was a disappearance,
it was calm and amicable, yet
it felt dramatic.
It was classy, yet it was cold.
It was all so very you.
So very you.

Rain

The rain taps
tentative like a stranger
Fuck off rain
Shattered smiles and kicked in doors
Tipsy but not drunk
I don't want to dance today

It rained on the day she died
and somehow I can't forgive it
Or anyone
Blue lips and rag doll eyes
Meaningless drips
puddles of life evaporating

It didn't rain the day of her funeral
the weather man said
That makes sense
I hear her voice through the letterbox
Occasional whispers
when the old house sighs

Her Ghost

When the light is swallowed up
there is only her ghost for company
in the darkness and silence I still hear
    her voice –
words and words and history
while it remains too dark to read.

Just Another Goodbye

In the near naked light
of an undecided Berlin morning
I smiled and I waved
   goodbye
             as she wistfully walked away.
The taste does not linger
and the memory covertly fades.
Has she forgotten too?
   Now
the world jerks on unsteadily,
just as it always has.
Just as it should. I think.

The Empty Doorway

Imagination has failed me
when staring at the doorway
I can't make her appear.
No magic or music, no apparition –
she still isn't here.

Afraid

A feverish red light flickers
half buried in the darkness
distant on the oil black lake.
Smooth, the water whispers
but I am afraid.
Too afraid to swim,
not brave enough to sink.

My Town

My town   living town
tired town   proud town
warm town   grim town
dying town   leave town

Always town   we're free in town
impossible to explain this town

*A town that draws sympathy and scorn
in equal measure*
*People believe it should be absolved of sin
given a chance   granted redemption*
And why not?

Old town   fighting town
drink in the last chance saloon in town
Mining town   mourning town
some people have lost faith in town
Town of *Kes*   striking town
brassed off with life in town

Political town   hate's around
the sound of marching boots in town
May is up   Corbyn's down
there's an awful purple threat in town
Red town   Labour town
it feels like it's a forgotten town

Howling town   physical town
Line after line serenading town
   Local town   global town
Downbeat lovers in this dreaming town
   Market town   drinking town
Downing shots and singing songs in town

   Lust in town   showing flesh in town
red raw flesh when it's hot in town
   Sunny town   dirty town
is it nice to be back in town?
   Breathing town   weeping town
people on their knees in town

   Builders town   artists town
boys in bands about in town
   Poets town   junkies town
hard to be a saint in town
   Violent town   damaged frown
choreographed rioters dance through town

   Ghost town   shadow town
sometimes I hear your voice in town
   Life in town   death in town
just watch the world go by in town
   We're free in town   free in town
there's a chance to truly be in town

> *Give me art and poetry and madcap music*
> *Give me football and pints and union banners*
> *Give me fanzines and brass bands and pork pies*
> *Give me fry ups and moors and pensioner scooters*
> *Give me charity shops and pit villages and cricket in*
> *the summer*

Give me graffiti and socialist slogans
and first-time love
Give me the sound of trainers slapping on concrete and
the confidence of youth and the dreams of a visionary
Give me space and smiles and give me hope

Historic town   still standing town
my town   my town   my town

English Summer, 2021

the shameless empire / lost
exceptionalism and dust / ashes
blood soaked flags / sighs
nobody likes us / yet
we do care / inadequate
rage bottled up / divided
rage spilled out / broken
men as meat / hopeless
God save the / hopeful
no saviour here / only
madness and sadness / butchered
Brexit Britain banality / philistines
shout the loudest / escape
there is no / escape
there is this / disillusion

The Sound of Fear

The sound of fear
isn't an easy noise to describe
It isn't an easy noise
to listen to
A high-pitched whine or squeal
that comes from a place deep inside
the human body   where the human mind
has only loose and fleeting
control
Sometimes it comes out
as nothing more than a sad uncontrolled whimper
If you hear the sound of fear
you won't forget it
That sound can cause
a physical reaction in even the most
world weary souls
Fear as sound
awful   visceral   unnatural
So understand please
my own fear and my own sticky glumness
as I watch the world change
The sound of fear
may become the sound of these times
Of that   we should all be scared

Welcome to Town

Full moon or not,
cloudy or clear skies,
the heels are out in force tonight
making music on the cobbles as they go.
Females flocking to the spot
where males keenly wait,
refreshing and jostling
for the prize, for the right.
Not quite described as nature
but natural in these times,
masked and with seasonal feathers
the females arrive.
Scholars lurk in shadows
listening, watching this ritual
pass them by. This is not their time.
Cheap perfume and illegal substances,
electric soundtrack to boot.
The mystery remains silent
when the obvious game is being played.
The dancing fills in for courtship
and shot glasses are memories past,
this 21st century ritual
was never made to last.

Where it Flows

There was dried blood on the toilet seat
The human detritus of hours of digging
desperately inside rotten groins
trying to find where it flows

There isn't much else left of him now
A pair of dirt encrusted trackies
that he would wear in rotation with his only other pair
and letters from probation about appointments

There's nothing else to do apart from bag them up
A life that once contained hope
with a woman and children and
dreams of something better than this empty room

Sparse   life is often so sparse

There is almost a feeling of life and death on repeat
Sitting thinking as the waves break pointlessly
against the rocks and where a creek meets the sea
listening listening listening
where it flows

Second-hand Camera

This old second-hand camera
has seen more than I have.
It caught time that no longer exists
but it couldn't keep hold of it.
It doesn't have that kind of grip.
Beauty and pain;
this camera was there.
It sits lonely now, gathering dust
and I wonder briefly;
who was with it
in those hours that danced away?

Drunken Courage

Drunken courage
I know that ailment
My sober frailties ruthlessly exposed
in a melting mist
of male pride and heavy flung hands

I drink till I drown
to ease my mind
and quieten some of these voices
This company of crackpot mirages
that I never invited here

Drunken courage
I know that ailment
Suddenly speaking up about me
about you about chances and destiny
in the shadow of long desperate odds

I drink till I drown
to ease my mind
and it used to work so brilliantly well
This heavy attack on my own wits
that somehow stood me up

Now I'm not sure about any of it
Drowning my sorrows but the tide isn't right
The sun hunkering down
somewhere below Valley Bridge
Where lonely people learn to fly

Drink

Dylan Thomas drank and drank and drank
Well   the history books are soaked

A grown man cried desperately
as he spoke of losing control
of drinking and drinking and drinking
of missing his hard-earned sobriety
   No great shifts or thunder claps
 no parting clouds and no singing virgins
   I helped him   sent him on his way to a meeting
   Cliché   one day at a time
   Yet as he left   my thoughts dived
under the surface   inwards

   Well   forget the history books
   I want a drink

Twelve Beers

Twelve beers seems excessive now
but at the time it felt about right
Just the puppy for company helping me escape
   the alcohol slowly loosening the shackles
   if only for a brief time
Next morning alcohol aches
   a speech to deliver
   hungover and glum
What is this world?
Ad lib a 'great speech'
   hugs and pats on the back
It felt good but in some strange way it was as if
   I'd somehow got one over on everyone
Then it was done
and I thought about the weekend's drinking
   and an idea for a novel

Upperwood Road

Stood in the crystal night light
beyond me only silence
and old newspapers
dancing on the winter breeze.
Voices ask why I am out here
though they are not real.
Still, they are taunting
as once I was looking for something.
Now in brisk solitude
it is impossible
to recall what it is.

The Rabbit on the Path

Crunching twigs
and the suspicious murmur of a dying breeze
are the sounds of the path,
the long straight path
of escapist dreams
in the shrewd woodland haze.
Never ending in the deep imagination
until it reaches the sea;
the hidden brooding sea
nearby though out of ear shot,
I long to hear it roar.
Solemn sunlight
pierces the scene
dripping onto the path,
offering hope with majesty.
Some birds sing
but more are silent and sick
for they have witnessed this before.
The past, where their singing stopped
and they knew
the future had been given away,
or perhaps lost at a card game.
Step on
avoiding the nettle stings
lurking at the foot of trees,
evil finds home in the shadows
and sin is never,
or very rarely an accident.

I long for something,
something to smell
or to touch
with saintly hands
and free sober considerations.
Still the path carries me
but it doesn't like my weight;
fear weighs heavy
on the soul of a lost man
desperate to be found,
to be kicked and whipped,
cursed and condemned
if it means
that he knows.
Does the rabbit know?
As it hops out of
the undergrowth, can it possibly?
We breathe in time
catching the rabbit's
eye and holding it
tormented and still,
frozen like metal on a magnet.
The breeze is silent now.
It moved away to another path,
another man who has a lover.
Whispering a different story,
the wind knows
nothing of loyalty.
It doesn't stop for love
or for war. It knows
only the entire world.
The rabbit moved dopily,
mockingly like it knew
of my abstract dilemma.

Death stalks us all
and I needed answers.
Taking aim, with the aim to kill
it became clear I was alive.
Powerful in so many ways,
yet in the end completely powerless.
Without love, you abandon
an entire space,
a part of the soul
where spite, loss
and troubled notions
are free to fill the void
and wreak an unholy havoc
on the desolate mind.
Love has to be important
and loss had to be reasoned.
It has to be.
Pulling the trigger
the young rabbit fled
but it left its body behind,
bloody and gaping;
a truly horrible sight.
Standing over it
only brought more shadows to the scene.
As said, shadows offer no answer,
only a breeding ground for sin
and fear and twisted nightmares.
Nothing was gained
when innocence hitched a ride
on the disappearing wind.
Step on
avoiding my own hollow shame.
Crunching twigs and a path to the sea,
walked on by eternity

and all her timeless friends.
It offered me nothing,
yet greedily I took from it,
the rabbit on the path.
If it did know,
the poor creature gave his secrets to the wind.
The wind blows away, so now,
I may never leave this path.

Seagulls on Green Fields

When the action is over
something quiet and reflective
takes over me   and calms me
   Chewed up earth sound-tracked
by the faint echo
of disappeared shouts
   On the next field along
delightfully green in the Yorkshire grey morning
  seagulls
   Twenty perhaps more walking and scavenging
for nothing in particular
   The hidden wind silently
ruffles the grass and the movement rivals the rollers
of the somewhere vast sea
   Blowing from the frozen north   creating rolling
waves of drizzled green
   They are a long way from home
these seagulls on green fields
   I think briefly   maybe we all are.

On Reflection

On reflection
I've never banged my hand
on the steering wheel
so hard or so often
before.
Does it have an effect?
In cold calm moments
a long way from the sneering roads
I sit and hope
not.
It was Badly Drawn Boy
who calmed everything down
though not with music but in
an interview about a friend with
cancer.
Madness giving way to sadness
sadness evaporating leaving only
the mist of numb cogitation
and slow midnight soul searching
silence.

Headlights on the Way Home

It was one of those rare days
where it snows but nothing shuts   the evening was cold
fresh
and the car was sticky with my own syrupy fear
I thought I would think of Donald Trump
and the new world we all now live in
but I didn't.
Like a flickering candle
dancing   I saw people flash
and disappear in the headlights
on the way home
I recognised these shadows
though I knew they simply couldn't be
who they seemed to be
It wasn't her
It wasn't him
The question as I drove
past white fields reflecting
joyless light was this

Who were they?

Manchester Airport Flight Path

With each plane that noisily disappears overhead
there is a feeling of being small.
A feeling of being grounded,
of being on earth,
even in the attic as the wing lights flash across the
skylight glass.
I don't tire of it – the 747 wake up call.
There's a mystery, a guessing game of where they are
bound for;
which borrowed red sun they will see set tonight.
They – the passengers
As the wings of the beast tilt I conjure images of the
smaller beasts inside
gripping their arm rest;
hang on St Christopher.
Why shouldn't I let my mind take that flight? (This is the
season of isolation)
Mind, thoughts, carried away by the growl of the engine,
snarling as it climbs.
Away from miscarriage monologues and seemingly
invisible invoices.
Drifting somewhere above the insomniac earth
and those 3am hours when the conveyor belt is broken,
the switch turned off by a tired God.

Crash landing reality bites
with silence for teeth
as the first plane vanishes over

fast flowing horizons.
The corridors of air are not mine today;
today the slow land will suffice.
Time to rise for doubts and chores
and all the visioning shades of stillness –
until the next distant grunt
becomes an approaching hum,
which migrates into an overhead roar – the next plane.
Another unremarkable day under the Manchester
Airport flight path,
please proceed to the gate.

Fool's Gold

Much thinking has been done since she walked away,
the process like a mine.
Mountains become minds and thoughts become the coal
whilst the all elusive gold
is the musing of the soul.
The unsuspecting victim was left standing,
embarrassed she turned away
because everyone knew it was a mistake
to sell the gold so cheaply that day.
The mining has stopped it seems
as the coal has become outdated.
Those thoughts hold no meaning now,
she is a figure from the past.
It was real, it was raw
and it left a hefty scar
But the real question remains;
Did we learn from the experience?
The sound of judgement is golden.

Sitting Green Man

I can see the sitting green man
from my bedroom window
    Alien green in the oil black night
  sitting zen-like in timeless contemplation
    Restless   I can walk away
but the sitting green man
                          never moves
    The same trees and the same blinding river of traffic
are all he can ever gaze upon
    Perhaps he is bored
    Perhaps he has some grander purpose
    Still   I walk away every time

Damp

The house is damp and cold
and sometimes, only sometimes
I moan.
Actually, I quite like the way
these conditions invade the house
and touch us.
Moaning aside it means we sense
and notice the seasons sway and change
which makes me feel human.

Red Admiral

Black coffee
a wake-up call of significant magnitude
and a cloud dappled northern sky
Cool autumn
a Red Admiral on October wing
and the smell of sad endings

So I sat and watched the butterfly
feed and flap
and wondered whether it knew?
Did it understand its lot?
Death, finales, curtain calls, last orders
the funeral march
How similar love and life are
in only the cruellest possible ways

I sat for a long time
trying to calm the churning stomach –
my own butterflies –
trying to quell the rebellious emotions,
feelings determined to draw blood and tears
Elaborate suffering
just one of a thousand chance catastrophes
surrounded by the sound of the whole world

That noise, indescribable,
of everything just being, existing
all around us and everywhere
From wind whispering through leaves
to distant waves
to two billion cars humming
to screams and sighs
to pylons buzzing
to doors slamming
to memories firing
to fires crackling
to gunshot snaps and mortar thuds
to dogs barking and wolves howling
to a stranger's footsteps
to a lover's moans
to carnival music
to the rattle of spare change
to the enormous rumble of the earth turning
to the tender chirp of Jasper Baby

To the sound of our love dying
To the sound of a butterfly's wings

Surrounded by it all in late October
The Red Admiral sensed something
and silently slipped away . . .
That future is a memory now
That thing that never actually happened
is something that I can only remember

Acknowledgements

'Welcome to Town' and a version of 'Fool's Gold' first appeared in *Cadaverine*, autumn 2012.

'Cigarette Smoke' first appeared in *Eunoia Review*, summer 2013.

'The Sound of Fear' first appeared in *Word Riot*, summer 2015.

'Second-hand Camera' first appeared in *Eunoia Review*, autumn 2015.

'Manchester Airport Flight Path' first appeared in *Iniquitous Glory*, winter 2020.

'My Town' first appeared on a poster produced by *The Coal Dust Arts Collective*, summer 2023.

After studying journalism at the University of Chester, Bobby Gant experienced periods of unemployment in-between working in bars. Finding himself with time on his hands, he began writing book and music reviews as well as his own poetry and short stories.

Upon gaining employment in adult education, drug and alcohol services, and – most recently – emergency accommodation, Bobby found himself supporting the most vulnerable, complex and interesting people in society. Being exposed to these environments, along with his own personal experiences, led to the creation of this collection over the course of more than a decade.

Bobby was born in Barnsley, but has lived in various parts of the UK over the years. He currently lives in Scarborough.

BOOKS

razurcuts.com

@razurcutsmag
@Bobby_Gant